AF444210

Prophets
of
Los Angeles

Prophets
of
Los Angeles

Bernadette McComish

The Los Angeles Press, *est. 2018*

First published in 2024
A Publication of The Los Angeles Press
Los Angeles, California
United States of America

cover detail / cover design by Linda Ravenswood/LAdesign
www.thelosangelespress.com
ISBN/SKU: 9798218419103

The Los Angeles Press
Cover Layouts @bogglle
Colour Correction @bogglle
Cover Correction @corndog_patrol
Associate Poetry Editor at large Chelsea Rector
Associate Poetry Editor Matt Sedillo
Director of Special Projects Brian Sonia Wallace
Editor in Chief Linda Ravenswood

Dedication

For Roy Alnashef, who will not forgive me

For Roy Alnashef, who will not forgive me

Table of Contents

Origins

Crashing together
was easier after your
palm molded my thigh

under your hands
my body an ink valley
you've been drawing

you made me
curved with roads
through our sketched lanes

at night kissing you
I collar dawn
as Saturn's sixty-two moons

orbit the tracks of my violet heart
racing past warmer planets
to an infinite finish

Pandora

Prometheus didn't see
        her coming
        and when she was
        gone, every other night he welcomed
                whisky vultures to help his liver
                                forget immortality.

Easy   to say she knew   what she was doing,
blame her
for   opening. Even
with all the gifts
of the gods she could not   know.

She was not crafted
                from clay, not mud like Eve,
                she was stolen fire,
                        retribution dipped in Cupid's
                        poison, the perfect   punishment.

Even after the buzzard was slain, he returned
                        to the same rock and broken
                                chains, not looking for hope
        but for her and the home she kept
inside her box.

The Prophet of Los Angeles

He raised his head
forgot to take his pills
in half sleep stillness.

Weakly, he spoke to a god
he did not believe in—
lampshades piled in the corner
skins and drums in the closet.

Love, he said, *will not
find me here. I will
 rub myself raw into black
sheets
find solace in an empty room
and yield not to the sword
of a woman. She can wound
me
sing my favorite song
fall on her own blade. I will
plant her in a pot
by the bed
feed her morning and watch
her grow petals, spread like
lips without.*

*There will be no tenderness
no ice-cream, no movie
watching.
I will not shake her roots
or water them with care.
Her leaves will wither;
she is not fit for pruning.*

*When she grows back
into woman*

13

I will knead her until she is pliant—
bread for a feast of one
and keep her quiet in my mouth.

I will not eat all of her.
I will bring her into my belly
long enough to feel full.

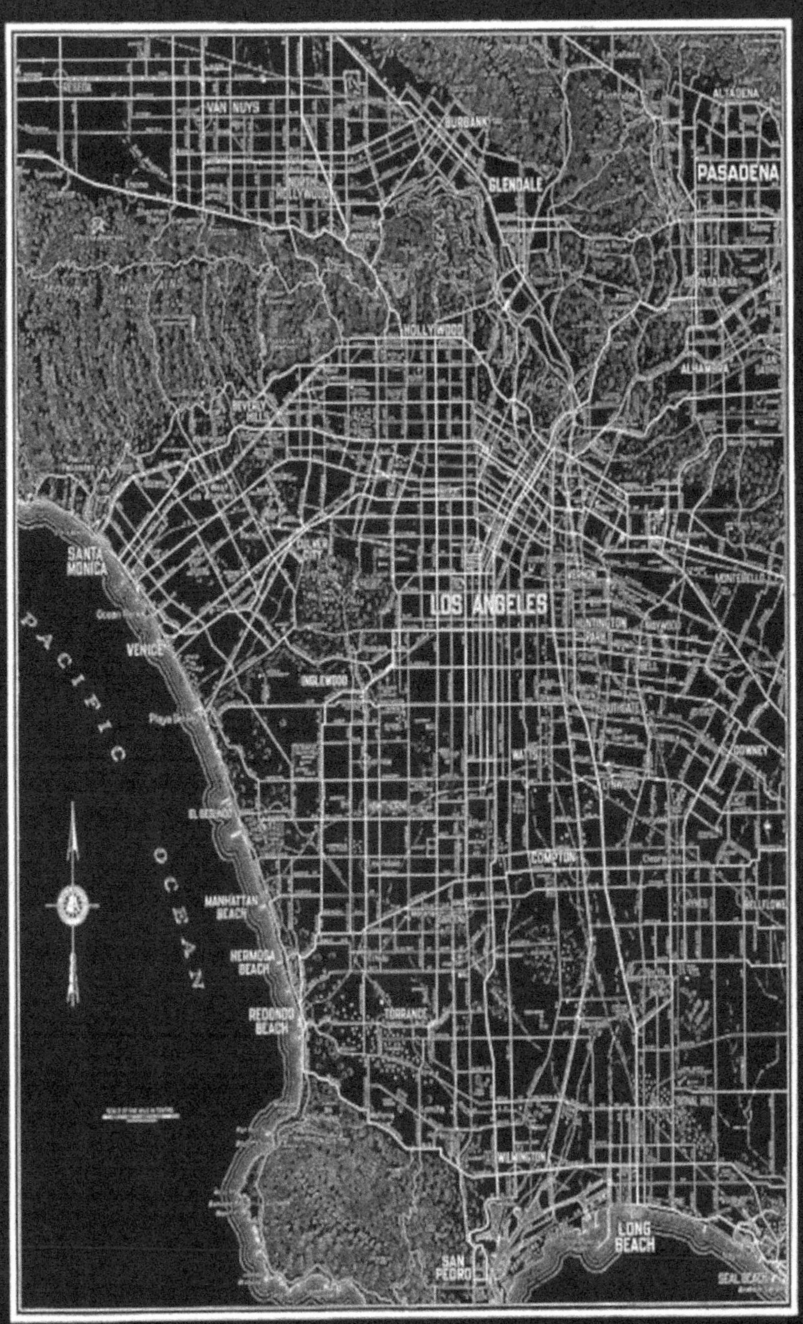

MAP OF METROPOLITAN LOS ANGELES, CALIF., THE FIFTH LARGEST CITY OF THE UNITED STATES AND WITH THE LARGEST AREA OF ANY CITY IN THE WORLD. LOS ANGELES LIES IN THE VALLEY OF THE LOS ANGELES RIVER WHICH BISECTS IT

Poseidon in Gin

How often do we offer
the earth shaker
a lime to twist in tonic?

He rules everything water—

it's not enough.

Our feet can't thank him
when we walk shores
so we tattoo anchors
to remind ourselves.

His strange mercy finds us
in sudden puddles,
drowning mistaken
for punishment.

He values sacrificial
horses and because our brains
are fluid he maddens them
beyond limits.

He sneaks in through throats
forces us to spill from eyes
and threatens to claim virtues,
plants a Pegasus in our necks.

In Aegae or a martini
he lives to drench
livers and lungs
until we return.

The Poet and the Pastor on Hollywood Blvd.

They hunt
        familiar stars, speak
        names on filthy
streets, complain about heat
and fame, hold hands, feet burnt.

The moon will decide
if they'll find home
        in his doubt
        or between her legs.

He abstains
        from touch. Her
        dress, cheetah print spots
open mouths he can
        almost taste as a city
        breeze lifts her
        sleeve or slit.

She keeps trees
        on a page
        wet ink stories full
        of sap, *the jacarandas
        of Los Angeles look
        nothing like the cedars
        of Lebanon*, she writes
        in a book she puts
        in her purse.

He preaches
        about the cost
        of love, the sacrifices
        made for stink
        on fingers, the affliction
        of being broke

beneath a woman.

She clings
to his voice,
        Where do I go? What do I do?
        I can't live without your...
he sings while he washes
his hands. She mistakes
lyrics for romance or prayer.
A poet can live in hope too long
        he says and licks
        her neck. Her nails dig
        at his soft, black t-shirt.

They confess under light
        polluted skies and kiss
        and kiss and kiss.

Zeus in Hooch

A woman in Tennessee offers a bathtub batch
instead of lighting candles on Sundays.

Her pleas to give birth to a Hercules
who will play for her favorite team,
be the hero in that song she heard in a movie—

only reach Olympus when 150 proof drips on the altar.

He wants to piss on the moon
with a mason jar in one hand
white lightning in the other.

It's been too long, he says
as he looks over the edge
of the atmosphere, narrows his gaze
as she bends to distill the mash.

She believes he will come
some night as a serpent, hawk, or bull.

He stopped making deals
with mortals, and drunk dials Hera instead.

Psalm of Intimacy

Silence replaced dial tones at the end of our call
	hang up, do not be afraid.

I believe dark tongues
in your head; my heart
	stirs green eye light.

I desire too many seconds under your fingers
	your gaze turned beneath me, beholden
	as you lived briefly.

I forget the friction of teeth, taste of skin
	your pulse thick with song and thunder.

I cry at my altar, sick with honey,
	ashen
	I pray for
	someone who fucks
	like you.

I wait on the ghost of us, head tilt to your beard in secret
	in this time of trouble
	your forbidden kiss
	an answer.

Hades in Single Malt

He doesn't pass judgment
like Lucifer and he does
not remove souls.
He observes, sits
on an ebony throne, a man
with his dog, waiting
for Persephone
to return from Spring break.

Unlike the Devil you've read
he won't be having a beer
with you or tempt you
to base things. He leaves that
to the buzzard gods of Mezcal—
something with a worm at the bottom.

On the rocks or neat
he drinks alone
while the souls of the world circle.

All descend, but still no one to talk to.

Psalm for Darkness

1.
In bathroom light
kiss me without violence.
        Afraid.

Hold me
        in your unmade bed
        make me better.

2.
In kitchen silence wait for water
        to boil, press fingers
in shadowed lamplight.

3.
I want to be loved
        tonight. Drive into midnight
        arrive on your doorstep
        leather dress, heels, lace.

You promise we won't last
        a pile on the floor.

Tell me
        a bedtime story

        *I will leave
        you damaged.
        The end.*

4.
You can sleep
        on my couch
        fireworks won't wake you

movie playing, you snore.

I imagine you leaving
        forgetting to lock the door
        but you stay,
        hard, and alone.

5.
In the half light of western sun
        you ask me to spread my knees
        on blood-stained sheets
        seep from my lips.

No man or god will love me
filthy like the R&B song you sing
        I can't get clean of you
        with drugstore soap.

7.
Never come back.
        I could live
        under you, barely
        able to breathe
        your maybe child inside me.

When you find a home
        lose the key
        to my secrets
        about dead friends
        about men in my mouth.

When you hold my face and kiss my eyelids
say you love me.

Postcard from Persephone

Dear Mother,

As the season enters December's mouth, I leer into the canal
of death, dip my toe to see if it freezes, if my immortal
self will cease. All those canceled faces pass and reflect
my eternal doldrums. Hades takes little interest
in my walks along Styx. He governs from a glass office,
comes to bed late, and carries on the façade
of "together." Behind our backs they call us dread and I can't
blame them. This barren hell is less than
a wasteland; it's like a strip-club with the soundtrack
on repeat. Sometimes I look twice to see if his horns
have shrunk, or if his skin has cracked in a new pattern
but he never… changes. I like to distract myself with Jesus and
adore
pictures you've sent me of saints. I try to invent new ways to lose
time. How much easier it would be to live among mortals, to find
faith
in books and candles. I wait for spring to return what's left of me.

Would you mind having Hermes deliver my sandals?

Psalm of Morning

I shall not offer my hand
as it trembles.

As bruises fade, I save one
        for you.

On the edge of loneliness, I fall from kindness
        my bones scattered
        at the foot of a bed.

Keep me in your mouth, between your teeth
        memorize my blood
        as a sailor maps seas.

Lift up your head and thrust open my door
        and without shame come
        within our hallowed bodies.

Examine the back of my knees, the hair on my thigh
        prove me worthy
        try my flesh beneath palms.

Wash your fingers clean and leave me now
        to seek salvation
        on the pillow
        where you slept –
        crumbled Old Spice
        on the sheets.

Ares Inebriated

A loaded Glock
a full shot—
That's American, he mutters.

No grin or grimace
just down the throat
and another and what

will they sacrifice to him today—
a goat, a village, a teenager?
Would it matter if they knew

he was over it, done with war
or would they keep killing
in his new names, the ones he hates.

At the only bar
in a town with no strangers
he drinks alone and thinks

It's 5 o'clock somewhere.

Occupied

In the wound

there is no future

of our opposing religions

my love is weighed

in time on the couch

in the bars

of my shower song

in the borders of ink

traced by my fingers

in the pints of ice
cream

you bring over at night

I measure us

by the volume of laughter

in the days

we don't speak

in hours spent

on the phone warring

over the value of

land, spells, and prayers

the extent I will go to

keep myself from calling

in the length of the
scar

on your stomach

our touch can be

counted on one hand

the sum of us

a mass of months

watching TV

a conflict

we solve

by saying

no

Cleopatra's Immortality

When you cradled
the asp to your breast,
did you ever
think the small uncoiled
creature could take you

away from Egypt? On the underside
Isis taught you magic, the names of each
deity and you returned, resurrected
Antony only to watch him die
again.

When Osiris came
you tempted his green
skin, and followed him
back. Your eyes forever
lost to the king of the living.

Psalm of Midnight

Shadows stretch
        as I find rest in the moon's pull.

The weight of a mother laid down
        in exchange for a lover
        who will not spend the night.

I lock the door as he leaves
        and smoke on the balcony
        a blue planet, Orion above.

100% Proof Eros

He doesn't drink because he'll forget
who to shoot aim at eyes by accident
which leads to lust and when it happens
Aphrodite must intervene
reap mortal agony but Cupid doesn't
misfire often and takes shots only
when longing for what's forbidden when wings
won't usher him to her naked he stands
in the doorway of an old wooden house
famished for what he gives to us when we
close our mouths and forget the name
of the after hours bar where we'd
wait for him to make a mistake

Psalm for Confession

I praise you with laughter
        a playlist of blues
        a vow you purge
        and refuse listen.

Forgive the terrible things I've done—
        lying to my sister
        not watering the plants

I forsake a new love
        for your fingers inside me.

My word crumbles
        as you follow me home.
        I believed I was a mountain
        holding firm against to sea of you
        able to say no, solid against the tide
        soaked alone.

Covered in salt and seed
        nothing can grow except abandon.
        My mattress is a wasteland
        snake skins, sand, gnawed bones
        a leveled land.

Bury me without a name
        without a tree
        without a landmark
        to fall on your knees.

On Which Goddess to Worship

Artemis will not get you laid
no matter how much scotch on the rocks
you leave half full on her altar.

The risk reward ratio
for walking in on her in the tub
is a limb torn per breast, and intestines
splayed for a peep between navel and thigh.
Her mood is like the moon.

Try Aphrodite for a while—

she'll let you look
she'll kill your competition
for a price.

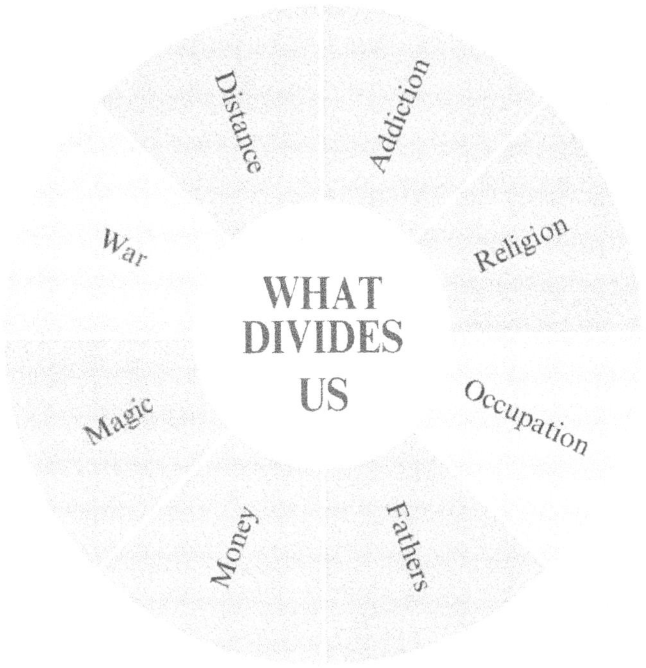

WHAT DIVIDES US
Distance
Addiction
Religion
Occupation
Fathers
Money
Magic
War

Athena in Tequila

Three shots
and the goddess speaks.

She transforms the consumed
into Achilles. Navigates
our bodies when we can't
remember the way.

Her
bolt—
fuels men

who hide heroes.

To swallow
is to worship
an 80 proof virgin.

She will leave you
wanting

a black hellebore
on your pillow to remind
mortals of poison.

She looks down
and says,

all those lovely goners
how they've forgotten
the old gods live
in spirits.

Summerland, CA

The wind is at it again, makes doors shake
the valley sway. She gives advice on wings
of bees, says, careful with hearts, and I ache
dismiss her, fickle goddess— agendas.

and my mortal mind ignoring signs. Time
is constructed by seasons, light, you say
it's early. How long before the bird builds
and her mate finds eggs warm, almost ready.

Break a sun, build a moon, make me blue
domes of life, stay as stone, keep your wisdom,
the wind will carry it if you don't move,
leave translations to the trees. A petal finds

me, lands on the page, I am connected
in whispers and what's left on your fingers.
My magic is stronger without concrete.
I hear my grandmother in shimmers on seas.

The dog sees you make me tea pluck a rose
keep the thorns, keep it whole I will press it
in books   memory for us to read loud
one day when distant and blurry, we can't recall

exact blue of oceans, color of clouds
behind the mountain only the pain
in shoulders, your salty back on my lips
your citrus tongue. Do not take it away.

Tell me what it's like to wake to my back,
a beauty mark. We still have the view, the light.

Stuck in the Second Ring

A tempest wracked my marrow—

fleshless, the bone splintered
and shrapnel trapped itself in your eyes;

this is why

I'm unseen.

The torrent so bright
blindness was inevitable, numbness
known only by those who can't resist
kissing—
the Lustful. Aren't we

above the animal? Creatures capable
of absolute kindness,
beings who sing

about how we long to be safe
from the precipice.

What Happened When You Didn't Die

They pulled you
soul soaked from the sea
your mouth and throat
without flame.

The wet ghost
of a woman latched
to your chest
spoke Heart and Beat
gave you back.

We're never the same
once the veil fails
and we see Valhalla
Odin in his tree
his eye full of salt.

And you—
one hand reaching for a branch
the other turned to sky
a red tail hawk calling your name.

And you—
speaking the language of the dead.

And your mother—
she wasn't there.

Isn't she the one
who's supposed to save you?

Her face before a flash,
before our grandmother takes us
to the tribe behind the electric end.
She was with a man somewhere

or yelling at someone behind a counter
she wasn't the one to breathe life
after enough minutes in the in-between
to make you a man without a flag
without a ground to call home.

Demeter in Grain

Angry at the one who resides
under seas, she bathed in a shadow river

washed her stubborn horse anger
and blessed those who glimpsed her harvest.

We walked on the High-Line singing break-up songs
she wore a green unicorn pin— an amulet

to protect against hesitation. Our purpose was unclear
our goal hazed by whiskey.

Watermelon didn't sober us and the ribbon wound
tight around her wrist was our only reminder.

When we arrived, all we found was an empty
aquarium, aspirin in the bathroom— nothing growing.

The Morning After

When you finally bled
and my fingers tasted like iron

you asked

what would mend
what was done

If the blood had not returned
could you meet my mother
My sister
My brothers

I said

only more blood
a push on the pavement
a tiny death
not even a soul yet

Casualties

Today, you exploded in my chest
other
a landmine buried in my core.

Why do we trap each other
take what belongs to no one?

If I gave you flesh
would you hate me
would you kiss me

promise it won't be the last time?

We touch noses
        in my kitchen
        in your bathroom
        on a bed
        a missile lights the sky.--

I can rebuild you better.
You could stop.
I could stop.
We both know how.

We made a date
for execution, stayed
long enough to fall
deep in a ditch dug by ancestors.

You will not be beaten.

I'll suffer us both
pay penance.

My grandmother warned me
about men like you
men who keep me
hidden with ancient languages
men who take
more than they should

men who make war.
You can feel guilty.
You can feel angry.
You can feel nothing.
I will love you
from shadows
from another man's bed.

This vacation from reality
was an oasis of short fingernails
and light licking.

I grieve
as if you'd gone
to a place beneath
the dead
where you say
there is no sun
no heaven
no ghostly haunt.

This divide will finish us
you
        stuck in dirt
        while I float in dream

where everyone I love
who died
dances.

You rot in the ground
unable to lift
the coffin lid
you built, sanded, and sealed
to keep you
from believing
there is more
          than veins, chemicals, and electricity.

You
          can remain remains.

I will continue
to call from above
whisper into scorched ground
I love you   I love you.

LA/HADES

× × ×  × × ×

My Grandfather's Death

(Part 1)

On the day my grandfather died
I dreamed we walked the shore of Jaffa
the green sea framing land I'd never see.

He said, *Home is*
and then silence
Where is home, I asked.

And he said something
I couldn't hear.
The next day

I tried to find a suit
for the funeral. I called you.
You offered your mouth.

Waking
his death
your lips—

It was all a relief.

(Part 2)

I don't think of my grandfather
when my fingers are inside you.

I like it better, when I'm in pain,
when all that occupies my mind

are memories of what I've lost.
I lose count of the days

since his death, lose the exact
color of white his hair turned.

You say I'm going silver and I bite
your hand as you stroke my forehead.

I blame you for his death
for every death. When I return

to your bed, I take
ownership of your body

like a city
or an island.

Once I am satisfied
I remind you

this violence
is your fault.

Terror (A Love Poem)

I want to escape
the fear
of failing at love

again. I made
a spreadsheet to calculate
the risk of you. Ones

and zeros next to each
attribute, a functional equation
finding the fracture

in your armor of black
silk and silver chain.
Found nothing conclusive.

I woke without you
turned the sky gray
this week. Someone

scratching through
the wall last night
kept me up.

We didn't meet
on a dark star
or in a vast universe

but in an underworld
of Los Angeles, in a castle under

construction.

Your demon made it rain
fire so I could find you
from the top of the tower

and I fell from a graceless
elevator into your long fingers.
I've been catching ghosts

in my free time.
They wouldn't stay
until I told them

prophecy, the one of you
in a casket. I am gray, looking
down on your death,

a portrait of us
above, your back to the artist.

I want to bury
my hands in the soil
of your skin

find home in the small
of your back, run
my nails down

your neck, breathe
dried flower songs.
Your tattoo ink stamped

a four-chambered heart
on my thigh. Bone
to bone let's be honest—

I've been broken, burned,
abandoned in a galaxy

on a dead planet
you found me.

Now, I get up before dawn, dig
graves for the street signs stolen
to keep anyone from following.

Absolution

If you were still a pastor

                Would you forgive me

If you were still an addict
meth burning your throat

                Would you forgive me

If you were a smoker
Marlboro Reds or Parliament Lights
like my mother
fingers yellow and sour musk

                Would you forgive me

In your rage
a black and white scarf
wrapped around your fist
your family dying in a land you'll never touch

                I know you won't forgive me

I call and say
      I'm sorry
I   am   sorry (you
know)

I tell everyone who will listen
in case they know you

sorry I didn't say no
sorry I wear a gold star under my t-shirt
sorry my son is not your son, sorry

      that I fell for your beard
      that I talked shit to a witch
      that I carved your name into a candle
      rubbed blood (I prayed wouldn't come)
           into a sigil
           the letters of your name

Sorry I didn't listen to your no
      called from a blocked number
      wrote you a letter
      mailed you a fountain pen

Sorry I never showed up at your door
the door of your mother's house

I wrote you a book, two emails, seven text messages

                you won't forgive me

You used me like a bag of powder
disappearing // reappearing

      I let you
      I liked it
      I forgave you

you said sorry
you wrote it
you took it back

you're not sorry

I forgive us both

in the name of the gods we abandoned
the same way our fathers left

Acknowledgements

"Aries Inebriated" and "Hades in Single Malt," *Flapper House*, Issue 15, 2017

"Pandora" and "On Which Goddess to Worship," *Rag Queen Periodical*, 2017

"Postcard from Persephone," *Persephone's Daughters*, 2018

"Terror (A Love Poem), *The Los Angeles Press,* V/3, 2019

"Psalm of Morning," *Minyan Magazine*, Issue 9, 2023

photograph / winona grey

Born in a blizzard in New York with the gifts of premonition and manifestation, Bernadette McComish is an educator and fortuneteller. She holds an MFA from Sarah Lawrence College, and an MA in TESOL from Hunter College. Her poems have been nominated for a Pushcart Prize, and have appeared in The Cortland Review, Deluge, Bowery Gothic, Indolent, For Women Who Roar, Slipstream, Storyscape, Flypaper Magazine, Waxing and Waning, Persephone's Daughter, Peregrine, The Los Angeles Press, Rising Phoenix, Reality Beach, Minyan Magazine, Kali's Moksha, among others. She was finalist for the New Millennium Writers 41st Poetry Prize, finalist for the C.D. Wright Prize, finalist for the Joy Harjo Prize, and winner of the 2022 Kali's Moksha Prize in Poetry. She has two chapbooks— *The Book of Johns* (Dancing Girls Press 2018) and *Florence Nightingale's Lost Log* (Lily Poetry Review 2021). She teaches High School in LA, and produces The Poetry Brothel Los Angeles. She is the immersive events manager at The Poetry Society of New York.

Titles available from The Los Angeles Press
www.thelosangelespress.com and where ever fine books are sold

a Jungle Refuses to Give Up
Frankie Tan, The Los Angeles Press, 2023
(Solo Collection $14.95)

The Los Angeles Press V9, The Gold Issue,
The Los Angeles Press, 2023 (Anthology $19.95)

The Los Angeles Press V6, The Dance,
The Los Angeles Press, 2022 (Anthology $19.95)

The Los Angeles Press V7, The Sacred,
The Los Angeles Press, 2022 (Anthology $19.95)

The Los Angeles Press broadside,
accompanying poster Barnsdall Art Gallery, solo exhibit, Olga Koumoundouros,
2019 ($19.95)

The Los Angeles Press V8, The Chain,
The Los Angeles Press, 2023 (Anthology $19.95)

The George Floyd Poetry Anthology,
The Los Angeles Press, 2021 ($18.95)

The Quietest of Wonders, Morgan Alise,
The Los Angeles Press, 2021 ($18.95)

Broadside, hand made, soy ink, Risograph,
Mikeas Sanchez, trans. David Shook,
The Los Angeles Press, 2018 ($18.95)

Broadside, hand made, soy ink, Risograph,
Chelsea Rector, The Los Angeles Press, 2018 ($18.95)

The Los Angeles Press,
V4, hand made, soy ink, Risograph, 2020
(Anthology $18.95)

The Los Angeles Press, proto zine,
hand made, soy ink, Risograph, 2015, ($20.00)

The Los Angeles Press   Upcoming titles for 2024

The Poet Politician   Anthony Portantino
Contact Boundary   Allegra Parks
Untitled   Kendalle Getty
Life in the Body   Rosalind Brenner
Dream of the Unicorn   Christina Cha